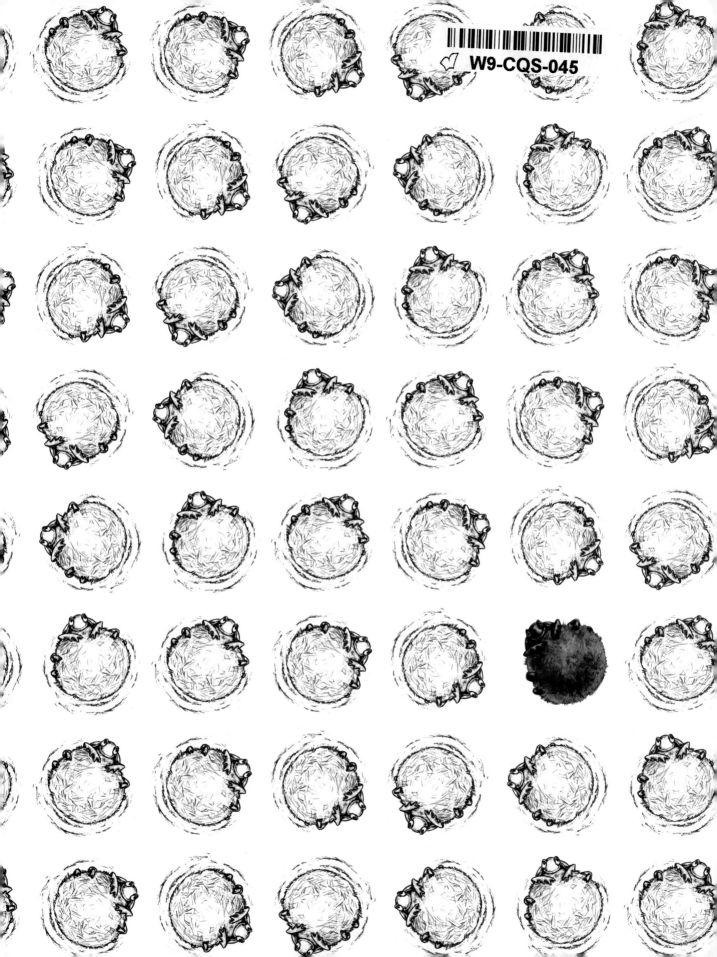

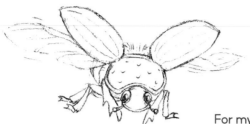

For my great-nephew Jackson Ray.
You are loved.
-S. R. S.

For Mom.
Your determination and spunk keep us rolling.
-M. B.

Pygmy
Giraffe
Publishing

Pygmy Giraffe Publishing
An imprint of Lyric and Stone Publishing
Phoenix, AZ 85050

ISBN-13: 978-0-578-93550-8
Third edition.

Pygmy Giraffe Publishing is committed to providing
products that are safe for our children and our planet.

Printed in China.

www.pygmygiraffepublishing.com

STEVE THE DUNG BEETLE:
ON A ROLL

words by **SUSAN R. STOLTZ**   pictures by **MELISSA BAILEY**

HEY, this is my poo!
Go find your own.
It's time to roll this poo home.

Hey, Steve!
Why are you rolling
that ball of poo?

Because it's my job to help
clean up the environment.
That's what dung beetles do!
Without us there would be
poo all over the place.

Oh. I didn't know that.

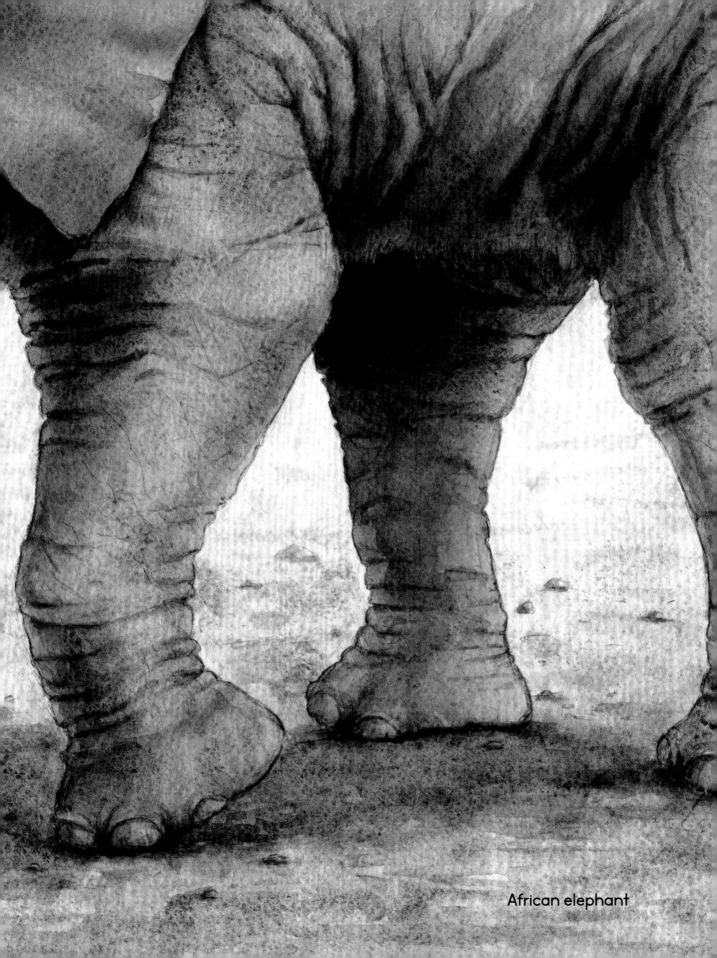

African elephant

Masai giraffe

Hey, Steve!
Why are you rolling that ball of poo?

I'm going to recycle this poo
and use it for something else,
but first I have to get it home!

Reduce, reuse, recycle.

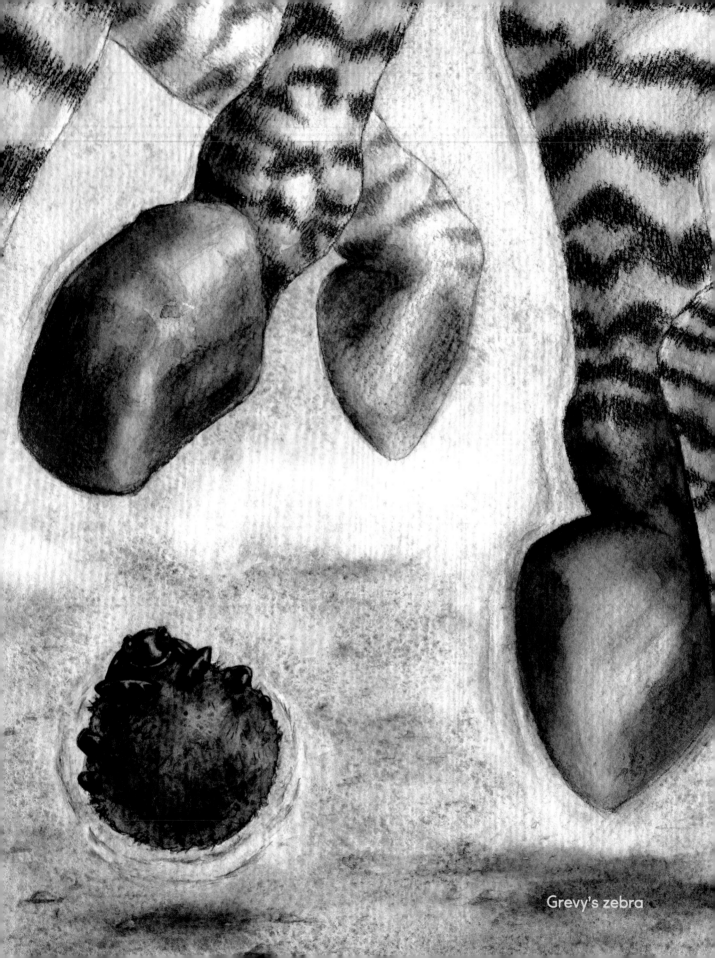
Grevy's zebra

Hey, Steve!
Why are you rolling that ball of poo?

Because when I roll it underground
it makes a bed for the baby dung beetles.

Yuck!

Hey, Steve!
Why are you rolling that ball of poo?

Gotta get it home quickly.
I'm in a hurry—can't stop to explain!

ostrich

Hey, Steve!
Why are you rolling that ball of poo?

When I roll it underground, it helps to
control the amount of flies and other
insects that bite and annoy you!

That makes me happy.

warthog

Hey, Steve!
Why do you roll that ball of poo
upside-down and backwards?

Because my back legs are much stronger
than my front legs.

Uh-oh...

African lion

Nile crocodile

Hey, Steve!
Why are you rolling that ball of poo?

When I clean up the poo,
it doesn't run into the water when it rains.
That helps keep the river clean.

Wow. Thanks!

mandrill

Hey, Steve!
How do you find your way home
when things are in your way?

I can navigate by where the sun is
in the sky so I am never lost.

That's amazing.

Hot! Hot! Hot! Hot! Hot!

Hey, Steve!
Why are you standing on that ball of poo?

The ground is very warm.
When I work so hard rolling this poo home,
my feet get burning hot.
When I stand on it, it cools them down.

Good idea!

dik-dik

Hey, Steve!
Your poo is out of control!

I know!
I'm trying to get it underground...
    ...whoops...
        ...to fertilize the dirt...
        ...yikes...
            ...and help plants and trees...
                ...WHOA...
                    grow!

HA HA HA HA HA!

spotted hyena

pangolin

Hey, Steve!
Why are you rolling that ball of poo?

It's my job to help plant
trees and flowers.
There are seeds in this poo.
When I roll it underground,
those seeds begin to grow.

That's a big job.

Hey, Steve!
Why are you standing on that
ball of poo and looking at the stars?

The position of the moon and
the stars help me find my way home.

That's fascinating.

African crested porcupine

Hey, Steve!
This poo is so delicious!

It sure is juicy.
It's the best dung ball I've ever rolled home!

What would we all do without you, Steve?

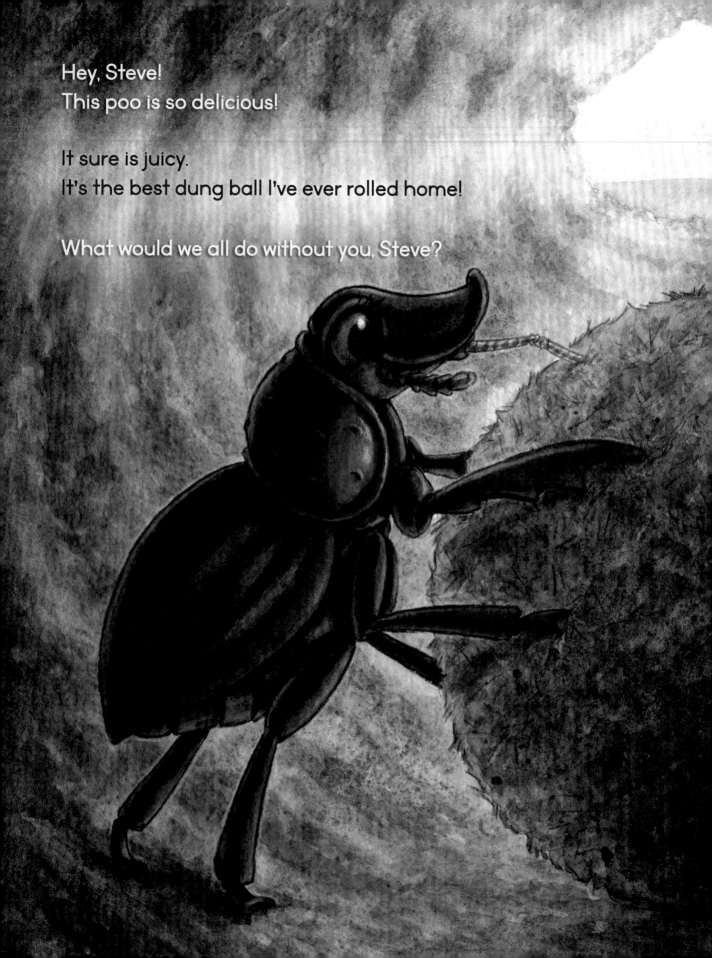

DUNG BEETLES

There are between 7,000 and 10,000 dung beetle species around the world. They are found on every continent except for Antarctica.

Why do dung beetles spend so much time rolling around animal dung? Well, poo is nutritious, often containing undigested pieces of food. Along with nutrients, dung beetles also get water from the feces of other animals, mainly herbivores like elephants, rhinoceros, cows, kangaroos, and zebras.

Many dung beetles will only feed on the dung of a specific animal species. And although this all sounds disgusting, dung beetles play an important ecological role in nutrient cycling within their environment.

ARE AMAZING!

When we think of dung beetles, we often think of a very small insect rolling a very large ball of dung (as is depicted in this book). But not all dung beetles roll a dung ball. Some species will tunnel below a dung pile. Some actually live in poo!

Dung beetles are small but very strong and able to move balls of dung that weigh much more than they do. Some dung balls weigh a thousand times more than the beetles themselves! Those species that do roll their dung ball often do so to supply their larvae with food. Eggs are laid directly in the feces and when the larvae hatch, they consume the dung.

C. Drew Foster
Animal Curator, Phoenix Zoo

SOME OF STEVE'S FRIENDS

THE PANGOLIN

Pangolins are the most critically endangered species you've never heard of. They are the only mammals covered in scales. Similar to birds, they eat small pebbles to aid in food digestion. You can see Steve pushing a pebble towards the pangolin in the illustration. They are the world's most unique and most heavily trafficked wild mammal. The pangolin is roughly the size of a small dog and is covered completely in scales made of keratin, the same material that makes up our hair and nails. There are eight different species of pangolin, native to both Africa and Asia, and, in particular, China.

THE SPOTTED HYENA

Hyenas look similar to dogs, but they are actually more closely related to cats. Their jaws are strong enough to crush a bowling ball. Females are much larger than males and are much more aggressive.

THE DIK-DIK

What is a dik-dik? It's a small African antelope that weighs between six and thirteen pounds. Dik-diks have long flexible snouts that cool the hot African air before it reaches their lungs!

THE AFRICAN CRESTED PORCUPINE

This is the largest porcupine in the world. The porcupine will rattle its quills and stomp its feet to scare away predators before it uses its nearly 30,000 quills. Porcupines cannot shoot or throw their quills; they have to physically poke them into whatever is irritating or threatening them. Each quill has a topical antibiotic, so a porcupine attack will not necessarily lead to an infection. This is a defense mechanism to prevent accidental self-quilling.

MORE DUNG BEETLE JOKES

What is a dung beetle's favorite snack?

A poopsicle.

What is the dung beetle's favorite number?

Number 2.

What does a dung beetle put on a hot dog?

Mus-turd.

Why did the dung beetle put on a swimming suit?

So he could go in the swimming poo.

What does a dung beetle eat for breakfast?

A Poop Tart.

What does a dung beetle use for his email?

A com-poo-ter.

HA! HA! HA! HA! HA!

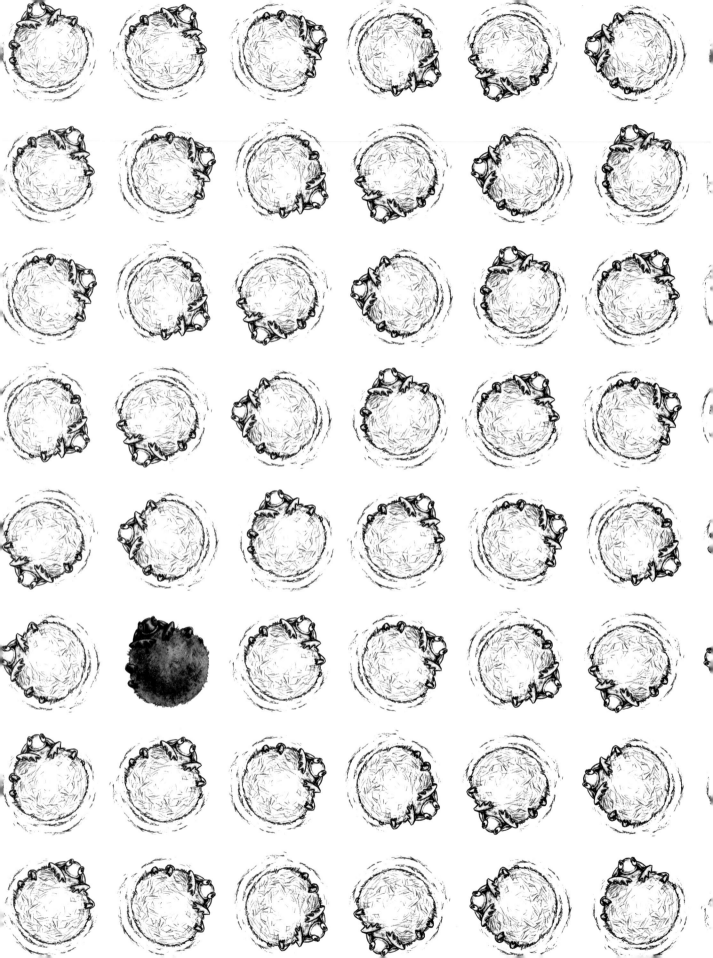